# You Should Be Free

by S. R. Brudlo

## YOU SHOULD BE FREE

First print edition published by Sasha Brudlo.
ISBN: 978-1-7779315-0-6 (paperback)
Ebook available

*For mom.*
*Wouldn't have been half as interesting*
*if it weren't for you.*

## Since you're about to read this, you should know:

This one is for the restless. The stuck.
The ones a little more lost than they are found.
Those who keep poem books on their nightstands
like bibles, opening the pages when in need
of divine intervention.

The poems of *You Should Be Free* were written with
no intentions, no expectations,
under the firm belief that no one else
would ever read them, and the absurd hope
that somebody might.

Although I'd like to say a little
something more profound,
this one is for me.
But it's also for anyone
who's ever been like me.

This one is for anyone who's spent nights
flipping through pages of poem books,
waiting for one to speak up, saying,
"I am what you've been searching for."

Sometimes, I didn't find the answers
to the greatest mysteries in the universe
in the cracks of other's work.
I didn't find comfort,
reassurance, or clarity
written between the lines
I so furiously analyzed.

So, I wrote this.
I came up with my own answers.
I created my own comfort.
And, somewhere along the way,
I compiled a whole book.

This is the bible I wish I had.
The older, wiser friend I didn't.
The answers playing
hide-and-seek between the lines,
waiting to be discovered.
This one—this one is for me.
But it can also be for you.

It is my hope that this collection of poems
sits on your nightstand
collecting dust, until one of those nights
after one of those days
when the whole world ceases to make sense,
and you're maybe just a little bit hopeless,
and you're worn down from waiting for a sign.

It is my hope that you will close your eyes,
flip to a page, and open them to find
the answer you've been looking for
playing hide-and-seek between the lines.

— *Sasha*

# The Happy Girl

Her mom would play the tape in the car
on the way to dance rehearsals.
Track eight came on and her mom would turn up
the volume and sing along:
"Watch me go! I'm a happy girl, everybody knows!"
and her mom said, "This is your song!"
and she became The Happy Girl.

She was promoted to co-chair of the household
one evening in ninth grade.
They moved the family across the country in the dead
of night against her grandmother's wishes.
Her song played loud and proud
heading into the desert,
and they made it to their fresh start,
and she became everything.

She was a superhero and she was a miracle worker and she was a bleeding heart and she was a brave face and she was the glue and she was the stick of dynamite but nobody noticed and she was a dreamer and she was a teenager and she was a lover of life and she was strong and she was shy and she was inquisitive and she was witty and she was the first to jump into the pool and she was the last to leave the theme park and she was sick and tired and she was only a kid and she was larger than life and she was The Happy Girl.

— *The Happy Girl*

I was afraid of vampires,

so I slept with the covers pulled up over my neck.

I prayed God would keep me safe, every night,

and I hoped for morning,

and I was relieved by the sunrise

(because vampires burn in the sun).

As I grew up, the nightmares came less and less,

and I stuffed them away in a box labeled "Pretend,"

and I've been scared to go back and look at them since.


I was afraid of the future, so I stopped making plans

(because tomorrow's never promised).

I became the chill one, the cool one,

the easy-going one, and it worked for me,

except for those rare times

I felt like being the stubborn one,

and it surprised my friends,

and I lost a friend because

it wasn't what she was expecting

when she first agreed to get dinner with me

back in October 2013.

I was afraid of being boring, so I became funny.

Said, "I'd rather be ridiculous,"

because then at least I'd be interesting.

Then, I was afraid of my friends

getting sick of me (because it's happened before),

so I made sure I was super independent,

and never asked for too much,

out of the fear they'd spend enough time with me

and see that, like everyone,

I was average.


I was afraid of not being enough,

but I never figured out how to get around that one.

It didn't fit in a box labeled "Pretend,"

or go away when I made someone laugh

or when the sun came up in the morning.


My fear sat with me, asking to borrow my crayons,

and I didn't know how to tell it,

"I don't want to be friends anymore."


— *I Was Afraid*

When I go home for the summer:

The table will be set for four,

my mom's room will be spotless,

and the driveway will be shoveled to the best

of my brother's ability,

and all these things will remind me of you.


— *The Sentimental Idiot*

I sit on the front porch

while a chill sits in the air,

and the street is orange,

and red, and brown.

A delicate wind passes through

every color,

touches my face,

turns my nose pink,

causing me to brush the hair out of my eyes.

On this day, I think of dancing with you

in the driveway,

falling into a pile of leaves,

and I miss you.


— *That First October*

Doesn't it make you sad to think
that there are some people
you will never have a beer on the back porch with?
There are some people
you will never play board games with,
or dance with,
or drive across the country with.
There are some people
you will never call
from your apartment,
you will never say "I love you" to,
and never get mad at,
and never have a reason to.

Isn't it sad that
some people
will never question your life decisions,
will never even talk about them with you,
and won't ask you if you're sure you're going to
graduate on time
and won't tell you to go to work when
you don't feel like it?

There are some people

I would jump canyons

to have tell me they're proud of me,

or even that I'm wrong.

There are some people

who I will never disappoint,

and that is disappointing,

because that means

we will never have that moment of redemption,

reconciliation,

or any moment at all.


It makes me sad to think

that there are some people

I will never have a beer on the back porch with.


Never sit together, making fun of

those who claim

that Jesus only drank metaphorical wine,

and how they will never enjoy heaven

as much as he does.


— *Beer on the Back Porch*

Dirt and slush disrupt the perfect scene.

Because the air no longer bites my face,

I walk along the lake again,

which is quickly, slowly, changing from vast white

to patches of black, blue, and green.


It rains, and the world is clean again.

I should be happy.


I should be happy,

but I miss you.


— *March or April*

You will miss them. You will miss them at Christmas. At college when you get dropped off and they should have been there. You will miss them sporadically, crazily, momentarily, and randomly. At choir performances and dinners with friends' parents and trying to fix your computer problems. When your roommate hates you and when you're enjoying a cup of coffee in the morning. You will not always cry in these moments. You may even smile, all the more when it hurts. You will get used to missing them. You will never get used to missing them.

— *What No One Said to Me*

I walk through the parking lot

when the first snow starts to fall,

and I am happy.

The trees lining the street outside our house

are no longer colorful,

but ice,

as if they had been taken from

some ageless land inside a wardrobe.

Still, I think,

"This time, four years ago,

was the day I lost you,"

and I miss you.


*— December 17th-ish*

Your life is going to be harder than you thought.
You're gonna have to get used to being hit with bricks
of grief at seemingly out-of-the-blue times.
Life will have to be lived knowing that,
and you could cry one night after a really good day
just because you miss him,
even though it's been five years.

But there is good news.
Because true grief lasts a lifetime,
it has space to spread itself out.
You won't be suffocated under an unbearable pile
of grief for the next five years until you "Get Over It."

Some days you will feel all better,
others will make you hate the sunshine.
There will be seasons in your life
with more bad days than good.
There will be seasons where the good days reign.
With time, we learn how to make our way through.
Most importantly, we learn nothing lasts forever.

— *Bricks*

With its heavy air,

and vibrant trees,

deep green grass that goes on infinitely.

We soak in the humidity

at your brother's trailer

and we talk about you over beer and hot dogs,

and we miss you.


We go to the lake to say goodbye.

And I know you are not here,

in those ashes or those bottles

or that lake

or this summer,

but you should have been.


— *Most Likely August*

Let me tell you something true about grief:
Time does not heal it.
Time changes it.

But it's better that way.
Nobody tells you it's normal for your heart
to never regenerate new cells,
to fill the hole that was punched in it
with scar tissue.
But this is natural.

And grieving will feel different ten years from now
versus two years from now,
and those who've never grieved
will never understand
that you don't miss him any less
just because you can admit
it really does get better.

— *Pathophysiology*

# The Madness

The following pages take a peek
at the slow slip into madness.
The unwelcome guest, "Just stopping by."
The afternoons spent lying on the couch
wondering if you're actually insane.

You are not mad.
No more so than any other human
who has had to navigate this world.
You are not an anomaly.
Rest assured, and be comforted
by the fact that you are simply,
most certainly,
alive.


— *The Madness*

I'm trying to think of this as an underwater cave

that's right before me.

I want to make it to the other side, and

I know that I will, but

I am just beginning my journey.

Right now, I am walking into the darkness.

I am descending into the water,

and I don't know how far down it goes

or how long I will have to

hold

my

breath.

I do know,

however, that

at some point I

will reach the bottom.

I will make my way up,

out of the water, out of the cave,

emerging to find that I've made it after all.

— *The Cave*

I'm so used to being scared of the future,

that it's starting to come across as

cool, cucumber indifference.

— *Cucumber*

The perfectionist lies

awake again

thinking about how she's going to do

her next thing

just right,

so if someone claims that she's not

all she seems to be,

she can point them to the proof.


The perfectionist tries not to worry

about little dents in the imagery,

but always finds the one flaw

that causes her to rip up the paper

and start over from scratch,

because perfectionists don't make mistakes

as long as the evidence is destroyed,

and a blank page is so much easier to ~~deal with~~ handle

than one that's been marked up,

scratched out,

and scribbled on in fury.

The perfectionist rides a wave of inspiration

until she's almost said what she has to say,

but crashes on the shore of a deserted island

where nothing new grows,

and just can't come up with the right

line.

So, the thought sits only in her mind,

forever

wasting potential,

all because she was too afraid to make a mistake,

or worse, write down a cliché.


The perfectionist hides her insecurity

under a njhgbkd of carefully crafted words

and nauseatingly picturesque moments

far removed from the real world,

so that whoever looks

will catch only a glimpse

of who she most wants to be.


— *The Perfectionist*

Every so often,

I want to be the kind of person

who wears sweatpants

and people ask what's wrong.


— *Sweatpants*

You try so hard to be perfect and expect to disappoint people, even though your work is impeccable.
You worry about never being good enough. Why?
Time and time again, you have stunned the world with the ways you go above and beyond.

— *You #1*

Some days,
you miss two and a half
of your three classes.
Some days, you decide not to complete
your half-finished homework.
Some days, you don't do anything,
but feel like you've climbed a mountain.

Some days, you wake up wishing
you didn't have to do anything.
Some days, you wake up dreading
the nothingness in front of you.
Some days, you feel like half a person
with the whole world against them.

Some days, you don't feel confident, flirty, or fun.
Some days, you feel difficult.
Some days, you feel like everyone else
is the most difficult person on the planet.

Some days are just hard. That's the madness of life.
Some days you smile so big your face is sore, and
some days you can't fall asleep and it's four a.m.
and you cry for everything life is not.

You think you don't want to be alive,
but what you really want
is less of the hard days
and more of the sore-faced days.

— *Some Days*

Not everyone cries on the couch to their roommate
because they feel like they're losing their mind.
Not everyone understands that kind of hell.
Tell me, have you ever actually, seriously
questioned your sanity?

— *The Slow Slip*

First step, acknowledge that not everything

is in your control. It never was.

Look at the situation for what it is.

Okay, you wanted to enjoy your senior year of college;

you have depression.

You wanted to make lemonade;

you have oranges.


— *How to Make Lemonade*

You look for signs
in stormy weather.
You tell yourself,
"It gets better."
You run around
as if you're high
on life. Truth is,
you wonder why

it's still raining
on your parade.
The light you had
begins to fade.
You haven't danced
in forever,
but you have faith
that it gets better.

You tell yourself,
"It's just a phase."
Your mom agrees,
"Kids these days."
Your family friends
think they're clever,
pat your back,
say, "It gets better."

You wish they wouldn't try to rush it.
You grab the silver lining, crush it.
You thought
that was the happy ending,
but it wasn't.

"It gets better."
"It gets better."
But what if it doesn't?

— *It Gets Better*

31

"Do you feel like harming yourself?"

Just one of the questions doctors ask you
when you're depressed.
"No," I say,
but I spend the whole day wondering
whether or not I want to die.
I feel like I should,
but I don't think I do.
Whatever I feel is similar,
a cousin of Suicidal,
with tastes reminiscent
of being at the end of one's rope.

What I feel is sad. What I feel is heartless.
What I feel is killing me.
I feel like I should, but I don't.

"No."
I don't want to die
—I want to live.

— *Things Doctors Ask*

I have the world.

I have the world,
but some days
it doesn't feel like enough.

— *The World*

They say you can't see depression,
but I do.
I see it when I don't see you in class,
or when I do, but you have nothing to say.
I see it in your waistline,
in your smoothie which was the only thing
you could eat today.

I see it when you get mad at Disneyland,
and walk around the park crying.
I see it in your dwindling creativity,
your cynicism, your writing.

I see your depression when you pass by on the
crosswalk
and can't even bring yourself to say, "hi."
When you look up for a brief second,
a brief smile, a side-eye.

I see it in your anger, your impatience,
your erratic tears.
It may be invisible to some, but to me,
it's crystal clear.

They will try to say you can't see depression,
but you can.
I do.

— *The Invisible Illness*

I will always remember you fondly,
as the friend who held my hand as I was
crying in Disneyland.

— *Love #1*

# Stronger

This chapter is for the fight without an end in sight.

When it almost kills you,

but you somehow get through.


It's what lies on the other side of that semicolon.

It's like a phoenix rising from the ashes, but it's you.


It's for the war that feels unwinnable.

You were never a fighter, but you fought like hell.

And here you are.


— *Stronger*

Once upon a time, I thought love was simple,
something that came naturally to everyone.

When I first heard them say they hated their parents,
I was appalled.
When I first liked a boy who didn't like me back,
I was in shock.
When I first lost a friend,
I assumed we still loved each other,
until she showed me what cold felt like.

When I tried to be the best version of myself,
when I loved those around me
like we shared the same skin,
I was disappointed by the lack of love I received back.

When I finally found love outside my childhood home,
I was tentative.

Once upon a time, I found that love was not simple.
I found that love was not perfect,
but it was beautiful anyway.

— *Happily Ever After*

You have so many
incredible,
wonderful
things about yourself,
if this is how you have to be flawed,
that's fine.

*— Flawed*

Hop out of bed today like you got eight hours of sleep.

Like you already know what's going to make your day.

Like the world is a happy place.


Dance in the rain today

like you don't mind getting wet.

Like it didn't just rain two days ago.

Like you'll never taste water again.


Skip down the street today

like you just got out of class.

Like you don't have a care in the world.

Like you want to be alive.


Watch the leaves fall today

like you've never seen colors before.

Like you've just seen the love of your life walk in.

Like it'll all be gone tomorrow.

Reach for the stars today

like you can actually see them.

Like there's a chance

the lead singer will touch your hand.

Like they're not too far away.


Get out of bed today

like it's the first day of the rest of your life.

Like you've never had a bad morning.

Like you finally feel okay.

Get out of bed today.


— *Hop Out of Bed*

He's gone, and you probably wonder
if he can see you and your family now,
and if he's sad to be away from you at all,
even though heaven is a place where no one is sad.
You wonder if it's possible for him to miss you.

The worst part of "He's gone" is that it means
he will still be gone tomorrow,
the day after that, next year,
five years from now,
and up until your dying breath.
The part of your life with him in it is over.
Now begins a new chapter of your life, without him.

He won't be there tomorrow,
or on your graduation day,
or on your wedding day.
Your kids won't call him "Opa." You won't get
to have that beer together on your porch.
The future you had planned out used to include him,
and in a matter of one day,
he is no longer part of it.

But you will smile. Possibly
as soon as the day after he died.
You will laugh and talk and cry with your family.
You will have some of the best days of your life
long after he's gone.


My hope for you is that you get excited
for the rest of your life.
Because you are going to find good, worthwhile things
on the other side of this heartbreak.
You will find love and happiness so great that
it overflows from your spirit
into the world around you.
You will be so fucking whole. Just you wait.


— *What Else No One Said to Me*

There are stars you'll never reach,
nights when praying won't bring peace,
and words will make you bleed
before they settle your mind.
There are failures up ahead
that you haven't got to yet,
but there's no reason to dread—
I think that you'll find

There are trials worth the pain,
there are dark days worth the rain.
There's what you lose, and what you gain,
and there's always a reason
for the heartaches that upset you,
and all the dreams that left you.
We can't change the outcome, but we get to
choose what we believe in.

There's no way around defeat,
and sometimes winning's bittersweet.
Though you're standing on concrete,
there will always be cracks.

There are shades of misery,
reasons you cannot yet see.
Maybe the thunderstorm will be
what gets you back on track.

Remember where you've been
when the walk gets smooth again,
and when your uphill climb begins,
I hope you are aware
that there are journeys worth the risk,
days ahead worth all of this.
There are some places worth the trip
that you won't see till you're there.

You have kingdoms left to build,
and home movies left to film.
If you don't, then no one will,
so you've got to be brave.
And when disappointment finds you,
and the sun's so bright, it blinds you,
I hope every breath reminds you
of the trials you overcame.

— *Trials*

I always thought a book that was a little
beat up and worn out held more value.
This was a book that had been dearly loved.


— *Dog-Eared Pages*

# The Wanderer

That fire in your soul that keeps you

chugging along the track.

That relentless whisper, saying,

"You'll never know if you don't try."

You embrace every ebb and flow of life

and you find your way to magical new beginnings.

You run to the edge and jump into the sea

and you find your place in this world.

Not that you were ever really lost.


— *The Wanderer*

Sometimes, I like travelling,

but sometimes,

I just want to make the place I'm in

as wild and beautiful as possible.

One day I'll crave new places,

the next I'll wonder why I'd ever want to leave.

It makes me sad that there are so many

incredible cities in the world

and I can't live in all of them.

— *Cities*

You will be looked down upon by others for
your free-spiritedness.
People will make assumptions about you.
They will judge you for blowing off
responsibilities or being "too" something.
You will laugh at their naivety and tell them
you were nearly an orphan and
they still won't get it.
You will keep laughing as long as you're alive.

Because sometimes the pieces
don't fit together perfectly,
and sometimes stupidity
is disguised as loyalty,
and we all only get so many
rides around the sun.

— *You Should Be Free*

Sometimes, you've got to

make the choice

that feels right

and wait for the reason

to show up later.

— *Jump*

And the funniest thing happened once I got here.

I realized home could be a place
as much as it is a person,
or a sense of self,
or a dream.

And for the first time since I was a kid
I felt like I was home.

And I felt like I didn't need to run anymore.

Like I didn't have to explore the world
to find the one place where I fit.

Or piece together the multiple places
I somewhat fit.

Because this, I knew, was my home.

*— Home*

It was good for a time, but now I'm starting to see it was maybe never where I was supposed to end up forever. Maybe no place is permanent for me. This may not be where I belong, but it was another beautiful adventure to tide me over.

— *Permanent*

I want to tell my kids,

"You should find the happiest place on your earth,

and you should live there as soon as possible."

— *The Happiest Place on Earth*

You wish your story didn't have so many zigs and zags, but that's exactly what's served to make it just a touch more interesting.

— *The Thing About Plot Twists*

I want somewhere I can walk around barefoot,
not worried about being pierced by a piece of glass.
Somewhere I can dance in the kitchen and be joined
with enthusiasm.
I want to be loved by someone who sees no flaw in me
worth running away from,
who knows what they have when they have me.

I want to be loved so much,
and reminded of it so often,
that I never feel like I am wasting someone else's time.

I want to be surrounded by goodness,
safe. Shown that I am worthwhile,
valued. I want to be so happy that I am sad to leave,
and cry after it's gone,
not because it's still here.
I want to be free to be the person I have always been.

I want to dance somewhere
it is safe to walk around barefoot.

— *Barefoot*

Happiness is a journey.

The journey is the destination.

You've already arrived.


Welcome home.


— *Happiness*

# The Lover

This is not the part where I fall in love.
This is not the magical-first-kiss fairy tale
that ends with "Happily Ever After."
This is life.

This is the moment you realize he's not the one.
This is the crush that doesn't like you back.
This is the pain-in-your-heart, lie-on-your-bedroom-
floor, unsure-of-how-to-face-tomorrow kind of day.

This is you realizing what true love is not.

This is not the part where I fall in love.
This is where I make peace
with the almost's and could've been's.

This is life.

— *The Lover*

That moment that breaks the barrier

between other lives and our life.

That moment when a stranger in a coffee shop asks,

"Is anyone sitting here?"

In a matter of an instant, someone else—

some two-dimensional figure in the movie

that is the world going on around you—

goes from being a picture to being a person,

a tangible being who has thoughts

and questions and hobbies

and a life all outside of your own,

but because of that moment of intersection,

is now a part of your own.

Flat to round. Shallow to deep.

No one to someone.

Or how about that moment when
you're walking home from Starbucks,
and your roommate says, "Wait, is that him?"
You look up and, sure enough, it's him,
waiting on just the other side of the street.

You know if you don't at least wave or say "hi"
or *something*,
he'll slip away,
back to the other dimension
of being a stranger.
So you do it.
You smile and wave
and he nods as he skates by.

— *Coffee Shop Encounters*

The one who asks

for my number

before asking my name

probably isn't the love of my life.

— *Insignificant Strangers*

I want to know where you're from

and where you've been all my life,

and I don't want to write a story about it—

I want it to be for real.

Though I will, most definitely,

be writing about this moment for a good while.


Make me fall in love with you?

Check.

Mission accomplished, sir.

I hope you've been alive all this time

looking for someone like me.


— *Thoughts Upon First Meeting*

I thought I loved you;
I was fifteen.

— *Fifteen*

I'm just waiting for him
to casually bring up
his fiancée or
girlfriend one day.

— *Cautiously Falling in Love*

Of course I can

imagine a future

where I'm happy without you.

My life was never

supposed to revolve

around you,

and you should know now,

it never will,

but

I would love

for you

to be part of the ride.


— *Around the Sun*

We spent four years

orbiting around

neighboring stars,

never quite colliding,

though we'd often cross paths,

and I still think of the wasted time

and the things that might have been.

Love is…

When you don't want to kick your dog out of your bed,
so you say you're okay with sleeping on the floor.

When time doesn't matter
because it's never enough anyway.

*—  Love #2*

I wasted so much time

not being in love with you.

— *When You Know*

# Bitter

You will not be able to get through life always sweet as a Georgia peach. You will have days that leave you sour like a crab apple fallen on the trail. Dogs won't even want to take a bite.

For those days when you're the coffee that was poured before realizing there's no cream in the fridge. For those days your face muscles are tired of working so hard to smile. You will not be able to get through life always looking on the sunny side. You will sometimes stare at the sun in disgust.

This is okay.
You are human. You are not candy.
Let them spit you out.

— *Bitter*

Don't push me away and

expect me to leave you alone.

I love you too much to stay away,

too much to stop texting,

too much to not forgive.

So, fuck you.

Because even if

you don't return my messages,

I'm still here,

I still love you,

and I will never give up on you.

— *Because I Love You*

And I get that you're planning a wedding,
and taking seventeen units,
and responsible for fifty underclassmen,
but I still don't think it means you're too busy
to type: "Good! How are you??"
and hit send.


— *Left On Read*

I will always accept your apologies,
they just mean nothing to me.

*—  Sour #1*

So if I seem a little short with you,

it's because I'm hurt.

And if I don't laugh at your attempts to be funny,

it's because I'm worried.

I'm stressed.

I'm on guard.

None of this is fun to me.


I'm not mad at you.

I'm hurt.

I'm traumatized.

My life will never be the same.


— *On the Edge*

You made me look back and question

every relationship I've ever had, and I feel like

I don't ever want to forgive you for that.


— *Grudge*

The imperfections are what make something perfect,
except when the imperfections aren't perfect.

When the crooked smile is a little too crooked.
When the gap between your teeth is
a little too wide to be cute.

When the scars are a little *too* distracting,
and the blood is a little *too* realistic,
and it's scaring the children,
so they send you home.

Because they never wanted imperfections.
They wanted curated quirks,
molded to their specifications.

As it turns out, you're too imperfect to work with,
and you're not delightfully unique,
you're strange,
and you're not beautifully broken—
you're just broken.

— *The Imperfectionist*

83

Don't worry about keeping me happy.
I'm happy without you.


— *Sour #2*

It's pretty hard to fuck up chocolate,

but dollar stores do it all the time.

In this scenario,

are we the chocolate?

Am I the dollar store,

or is that you?


— *Chocolate*

I forgave you instantaneously,
but now I want to forget. This means that
next time I see you, I will not say, "Hi."
I might smile, maybe wave, but that is it.
I cannot pretend you were never cruel,
even though right now you look like a friend.

I want to leave behind that space in time,
the one where you woke me every morning
with anger in your footsteps. The one where
you took what was ours and made it all yours.

I do not want to be nice anymore,
so I'll gently back away whenever
I see you standing across the pavement,
simply waiting for the light to turn green.

Because to me, you are not just waiting,

you are interrupting my peace of mind,

and I pride myself on letting it slide,

while you pride yourself on everything else.

I cannot listen to you say my name,

and pretend you ever once said, "Sorry."


— *Forget You*

It's sad that you think I'm dependent on you,

because you take me for granted

when you live in that delusion.

I can live without you—

I just don't want to.

Contrary to popular belief,

I don't need you.


— *Delusions of Grandeur*

I never thought I'd be unfriending you.

— *Never.*

Because it has been proven

that salt melts snow,

only to be dissolved by its creation.


Is this the beautiful cycle of life,

or an unjust end?


Because it seems to me,

the salt simply did

what everyone expected of it.


— *Salt*

Don't apologize for saying my father's name
and reminding me that you noticed
when he was alive.

If you're going to apologize,
save it for all those times you step back
and shut up when any memory of him
is on the tip of your tongue.
When you shush your five-year-old sister
for saying, "I hate that your dad died."
Any time you think of him
and don't tell me about it.

Your memories of my father
will not hurt my feelings.
Losing him did that.
Your silence pisses me off,
and reminds me that I suffered
in such a way that
those closest to me
will never understand.

— *Your Memories of My Father*

It's easier to be wrong.

To admit your error and ask forgiveness.

To see what you did and fix it.

To be right involves convincing

someone else they're wrong,

or being forced into being okay with

never getting the apology you wanted,

and there is almost nothing harder

than changing someone else's mind.

— *Why We Surrender*

I let you think I was mad at you,

because the truth would've been worse:

I'm not mad,

I just don't care anymore.

— *Lie of Omission*

Be careful.

'Cause one day you'll wake up

and I'll be going,

and you'll wonder why,

but I'll remind you how

I've been telling you all along

what I needed to stay,

and you didn't care,

because you assumed you were my world.

So be careful.

'Cause all those stars may look dazzling,

but none of them will keep you warm.


— *Yours Truly, The Sun*

# The Loner

When you first entered this world,

you thought that things would be different.

You thought you'd be given a fair chance.

You thought people would be kind,

and you were disappointed when, upon growing up,

you realized this wasn't always the case.

The kind people seemed to be the exception and

the cruel ones the norm,

and it tested your sanity,

and it made you feel like the outsider

because you actually gave a damn.


You have always been good on your own.

You are the independent, self-sufficient, capable one.

You don't need anyone. You don't even want them.

Then come those nights when your window's shut,

and you've been lying awake for hours

and you think, if you allowed yourself,

you could desire company, too.

You could no longer be the loner

if you were brave enough

to try again,

and darling,

you have always

been brave enough.


— *The Loner*

I had a dream last night

we were still friends,

and I woke up with this warm and fuzzy feeling,

because somehow we'd rekindled the relationship,

and I'd forgiven you for disappearing on me,

and you forgave me for disappointing you,

and none of it mattered,

and it was like old times,

but the early morning fuzz doesn't last forever,

and now I just feel empty again.


— *Fuzzy*

And I can tell myself it's your insecurity,
and that you're losing out.
But at the end of the day,
I'm still the one who hurts.


— *Headache*

And after they've gone,

you wonder how much of it was a lie.

You wonder if they really were *only* late meeting you,

or if they really worked on all those projects

and really knew all those people.

You question everything they've ever said,

because once they've left you like that,

all you can see them as

is a ghost.

— *On Seeing Dead People*

I think your heart looks for people and wills them out of hiding, so when you see your friend from last semester at an exam, or an ex-lover at the drug store, *of course* you do.

— *Willpower*

**When I say...**

                            **I mean...**

"Hey I miss you"

                    "I care about you
                    and want to know
              what's going on
              in your life"

"HEY"

              "Do you care about me,
                or have I ceased to exist?"

"Hey, are you not getting
  my messages, or are you
  just ignoring me?"

             "It really feels like you're
                ignoring me, and I want
                    to hear you say it."

"Not accusing, just asking,
  because I don't want to assume
  you're just not talking to me anymore."

          "Please, tell me I'm wrong,
                  and have some legit excuse."

"That's what it feels like, though,
  so please let me know if that's not the case!"

          "This is my last-ditch effort.
                  Speak up if you actually care."


                    — *Olive Branches*

I want to go back, to the exact moment you gave up on me, and change my own mind so that you don't have to change yours.

— *Hindsight*

It's funny how quickly you lose me,

though slowly, bit by bit,

every time I feel disregarded by you.

Disrespected.

Abandoned.

Taken for granted.

And you almost wouldn't think

I feel these things,

even though I tell you I do,

because I am the carefree, happy one.

The one who is chill and childish

and loves life much too much to stay mad.

But you've always known there's

more to me than my free spirit,

so it's funny how you lose me.


— *How You Lose Me*

You're wrong. I took them so seriously.

— *Our Plans*

Your perceptions of me do not determine who I am.

So if what you're saying is that you need space,

I will leave you so alone.

— *So Alone*

You are the one who gives their all,

until you realize that everyone else gives very little.

You are easily disappointed,

discouraged,

disillusioned.

You use this as an excuse to be a loner when,

in reality, you adore people

and wish they wouldn't always let you down,

but they do,

and you hate them for that.


— *You #2*

I can't just sit and laugh and enjoy the moment.

I have to be afraid you don't like me as much.

I have to be worried because it's too easy,

because nobody stays the best thing since sliced bread.

— *Sliced Bread*

We are,

and

it is,

but

oh well.

— *Champagne Problems*

# The Optimist

I am a realist.

I don't expect the world to be good to me.

I don't believe in karma or justice

or even common decency.

But I believe in things bigger than what we see;

happenings we can't always explain,

simple serendipity.


I believe in miracles and conspiracies and magic,

and in sheer force of will,

and in pure dumb luck,

and I believe people can change:

Their minds, their behaviours, their attitudes,

their course of action when stuck.


I believe life is a series of mountains and valleys

and both offer a majestic view,

and yes, timing's a bitch, but it's also a gift,

because it allows you room to become

who you need to.

I am a realist.

I know the world is a big, bad place.

I know trusting others is often futile.

I know most fights are fought in vain.

But I am a realist.

I know there is beauty even in disgusting places.

I know there are seven billion people, and

statistically, I can't be the only one who cares.

I know most fights are fought in vain.

It is this word that keeps me fighting:

Most.

— *The Optimist*

But God is not karma.

When you slap someone in the face,

he doesn't reach down to slap you back into place.

He forgives and says, "Let's try to do better,"

no matter how many fires you set on this earth.

— *Karma*

Seeing you

for just three minutes

and talking to you

for just three minutes

and being flustered

for just three minutes

and remembering

for just three minutes

the magnitude of possibilities.


For just three minutes,

my heart yearned for the future

standing but an arm's length away.

For just three minutes,

you reminded me it still exists

in this big, bad world.

Just three minutes,

and I remember now—

I didn't always run

when things got hard.

I remember now.


— *You Reminded Me*

Somewhere along the way,
I figured out those things
were for other people.

Those Things:
Effortless friendships
Lasting relationships
Falling in love, mutually
Being the best in class
Being the most likeable
Being a first choice
Being noteworthy

I now realize I am not the one
who decides what is meant for me
and what is not.
I am just as worthy
of those things.
To everyone else,
I am other people.

— *Other People*

And it makes you think:

Even the romantic comedy heroine we idealize has to break up with her fiancé or lose her job or have a near death experience or fly halfway around the world before she meets the man of her dreams.

— *The Protagonist*

I don't feel sorry for you.

I'm sad because you lost your dad.

I hate that you did,

but I can't feel sorry for you.


Because you are not a tragic case, a child who lost a

parent and wallows in grief for the rest of her life.


You are a story about a girl,

thrown into tragic circumstances,

who overcomes the hurt

and goes on to live a full life.


You are an inspiration. Imagine that.


— *The Inciting Incident*

If you ask me for proof

that someone can come out on the other side,

I would tell you how my favorite color used to be grey

because I could only see in black and white,

but now that I see the world as it truly is,

I am in love with every hue.


If you ask me for proof,

I will tell you

that everyone feels

a little too miserable

at seventeen,

and braving the tunnel requires patience,

but once you set your eyes on yellow and green

for the first time,

you will not only see it,

you will feel it,

and you will know what colors truly are,

and you will never want to sigh again.


— *Proof*

I pray for many more years
of hating saying goodbye to you.

— *On Mornings Like These*

We are content.

What a wild dream come true.

— *Contentment*

# Ridiculous

For those who feel a little odd.

A little offbeat.

Who walk in the room and

hear the conversation stop.

For those who can't quite put their finger on

their place in this world.

If you haven't yet realized,

it's okay to be a weirdo.

It's

okay

to be

ridiculous.

It's okay if

nobody gets it.

As of now,

you are free.

Free to be yourself

without a care

for the opinions of others.

Free to behave

        exactly

   as

        you

           please.

Free to say

        exactly

          what

              you

          think.


Free to take the names they call you

                    as *compliments*

    and experience

          a life

that you

are thrilled

to live.


                       — *Ridiculous*

Yes,
I believe in miracles,
and I don't feel like arguing
with you about it.


— *Miracles*

I'm not sorry if I overshare.

You see, I once had a friend tell me

I was a closed book,

and since then,

I've done everything I can

to prove her wrong.


So this is why I am the way I am,

and I must say that

I have found it much easier to live

as an open window.


— *Freedom is a Cool Breeze*

She's the kind of girl who laughs

when she's freezing

to death.

Who wears Burger King crowns to prom

and puts her feet up on the dash.

She prefers chaos

over peace,

because that's where the fun is,

and she'll gawk at anyone

who tries telling her otherwise,

because she's the kind of girl who laughs

when she's freezing

to death.


— *The Oddball*

There once was a child who kept wild dreams
tucked away in her pockets, like colorful stones
found in the stream
by the field next to her home,
ready to go when the right time came.

She ran over to me and placed a dream in my hand,
smooth and untouched by the world,
weighing as much as a single lifetime,
glittering like it was always meant to see
the light of day.

And I promised that child that when I grew up,
when I had more control of my life and its situations,
I would give it my all.
I would chase after that dream,
and the child entrusted it to me and went back into the
yard to write another song on the swings.

— *Pockets*

My dream is not dying—
it is still alive and well.
Just like all of us,
it simply grew up
and changed into
something different.

— *Cancel the Funeral*

I need someone

who knows

that when I call them "stupid,"

it means

"I love you."

We do not have to forgive,

but we are able to forgive.

— *The Gift*

And how could you know me?

I'm not the same today as I was

when I stayed over till two a.m.

and wrote a blog about my faith journey.

I'm no longer your best friend,

and I'm sure you are no longer mine.

People change, drastically,

over the course of four years,

and I would never want to be that me again,

and I would hope you're not still that you,

because that you hurt me when she disappeared.


But please, don't get me wrong.

I'm not mad about this.

This is how life progresses, and I embrace it.


I can't remember the last time I stayed up till two a.m.

or when I last touched that blog,

and even our phone numbers have changed.

So how could you know me?

I'm not the same today as I was back then.

- *2 a.m.*

You say "Ridiculous"
like it's a bad thing,
but thank you.

— *And Goodnight*

I will never be a tortured poet;
there is too much life inside of me.
I will never be the girl who sits around
in the darkness
writing angry revenge songs.

I will bleed onto paper
but my blood is not auburn like sorrow,
like a brooding artist's.
My blood proves that I am alive.
Therefore, my blood is torch red.

I may very well be
that one kid
who's so damn optimistic
that they even annoy themselves sometimes,
but I will never be the one
who makes it to heaven
and says,

"Can we get some heat up in here?"

— *Tortured Poet*

135

Manufactured by Amazon.ca
Bolton, ON